Tell me about the
WORLD'S
RELIGIONS

Lois Rock

Text by Lois Rock
This edition copyright © 2004 Lion Publishing

The moral rights of the author
have been asserted

Published by
Lion Publishing plc
Mayfield House, 256 Banbury Road,
Oxford OX2 7DH, England
www.lion-publishing.co.uk
ISBN 0 7459 4628 3

First edition 2004
10 9 8 7 6 5 4 3 2 1 0

A catalogue record for this book is available
from the British Library

Typeset in Latin725 BT
Printed and bound in Singapore

Text acknowledgments
Scripture quotations are from the Good News Bible
published by The Bible Societies/HarperCollins Publishers,
copyright © 1966, 1971, 1976, 1992 American Bible Society.
The Ten Commandments on page 3 are from Exodus 20
(last commandment slightly adapted).

Picture acknowledgments
Picture research courtesy of Zooid Pictures Limited and
Lion Publishing.
Front cover: main image by Lindsay Hebberd/Corbis UK Ltd.;
side images from top by BrandXPictures, John Williams,
Michael S. Yamashita/Corbis UK Ltd., Alex Keene (The
Walking Camera), and Twin Studio/Circa Photo Library.
Back cover: all images by John Williams.

All illustrations, unless noted below, by Lynne Russell.
Map on p. 7, by Jacqueline Crawford.

AKG – Images: pp. 9t, 22r, 26 (Jean-Louis Nou);
23t (Erich Lessing).
Alamy: pp. 12r (Christine Osborne/World Religions),
17bl (David Crausby).
David Alexander: p. 14br.
Andes Press: p. 39.
Associated Press: p. 25t (Kamran Jebreili).
Helen Cann: p. 16t (from *The Lion Bible for Children*).
Circa Photo Library: pp. 15b, 25bl, 31b (John Smith),
41b (Twin Studio).
Corbis UK Ltd.: pp. 23b, 45b; 6, 31t (Earl & Nazima Kowall); 11tr
(Mug Shots); 11br (Rose Eichenbaum); 12l (Carl & Ann Purcell);
16b (Roger Ball); 17t (Howard Davies); 19b (Philip Gould); 24t
(Michael S. Yamashita); 24b, 28t (Lindsay Hebberd); 27b (Michael
Freeman); 32t (Paul Almasy); 34l (Alison Wright); 35b (Tim Page);
36t (Tiziana and Gianni Baldizzone); 37b (Brian A. Vikander); 41t
(Desai Noshi/Sygma); 43 (Blaine Harrington III); 45t (Dallas and
John Heaton).
Guzelian Photographers: p. 38.
Sonia Halliday Photographs: p. 18tl.
Alex Keene (The Walking Camera): p. 18tr, 29, 33b, 42t.
Lion Publishing: pp. 34b, 44t; 10t, 21b (David Townsend); 10b,
11bl, 13t, 14t, 15t, 18b, 19t, 30t, 33t, 36b (John Williams); 30b
(Joy Amsden).
Rex Features Hatami Collection: p. 20.
Peter Sanders Photography: p. 21t.
World Religions Photo Library: pp. 25br, 42b.
(r=right, l=left, t=top, b=bottom)

Contents

What is Religion?

Does Everybody Belong to a Religion?

Some people say that belonging to a religion is the most important thing in their lives. Others say it only seems important to them at special times, such as at the birth of a baby or the death of someone they love. Yet others believe in something beyond the material world – but they're not sure what it is. Some people say they do not have any religion: their ideas of why the world exists have nothing to do with believing in any sort of god or invisible force. This book will help explain why religion is important to those who do believe in it and what difference that makes to the world around them.

RELIGION TRIES TO ANSWER the important questions people ask about life and death and almost everything else:

How was the world made?

What is the right way to spend our lives?

What happens to people when they die?

Each religion has its own special teachings that explore these mysteries; they become the **beliefs** of its followers.

What people believe affects what they do. People celebrate their beliefs – or their **faith** – by reading holy books, meeting together in special buildings, saying prayers, and so on. These are examples of **religious practices**.

Young girls carry marigolds on plates and wear marigold garlands with traditional dress. This colourful parade is for the Dasai festival in Darjeeling, in India. The festival has Hindu origins, but Buddhists also celebrate it in their own way.

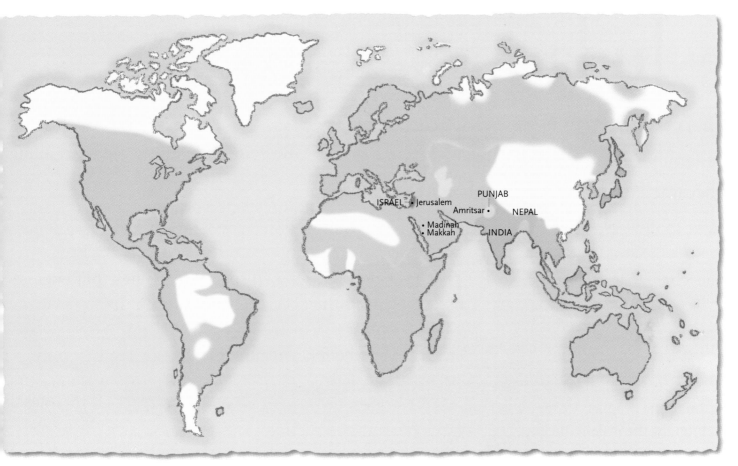

Religion is also about what people do in their everyday lives as a result of their beliefs: it is about deciding right from wrong and choosing how to live and how to treat the world and other people.

Judaism

Christianity

Islam

Hinduism

Buddhism

Sikhism

other religions/ not many people

How Many World Religions Are There?

There are hundreds of different religions in the world. Some are important in particular areas – for example, there are religions that are important mainly in China. However, a great many people all over the world now belong to one of six religions, and this book is about them. Judaism, Christianity and Islam are sometimes called Western religions because of where they began. Hinduism, Buddhism and Sikhism began in countries further east and are sometimes called Eastern religions.

This map shows the places where the six major world religions began – which is also where they first had many followers. Over hundreds of years the faiths have spread, and believers have emigrated to different countries. Nowadays many countries have people from different faiths living together. However, this map also shows the majority faith in places around the world today.

Judaism

JUDAISM IS THE RELIGION OF A FAMILY: a family that became a people. Before they became known as the Jews they were called the people of Israel.

A Jewish boy reads the Torah on a traditional scroll, here shown out of its scroll case.

Judaism began over 3000 years ago.

The father of the Jewish faith is said to be **Abraham**.

Later, the prophet **Moses** brought the people the laws that shaped their faith.

The followers of Judaism are called **Jews**.

Their important writings are the **Tenakh** (the Hebrew Bible), especially the part called the Torah.

Jews meet on their special day **Shabbat** (Saturday) in a building called a synagogue.

A teacher, called a **rabbi**, helps people in their faith.

A symbol of Judaism is the **menorah**.

THE STORY IS TOLD in the first books of the Jewish scriptures, the Torah. The book starts with ancient creation stories, in which God makes heaven and earth and everything in them. God's world is good and lovely, but soon people turn to wicked deeds.

In time, God chose Abraham to become the father of a great people. Through that people God would bless all the world.

Abraham had many descendants. Many years later, God chose someone called Moses to be a prophet to them – to give them his message. Through Moses, God gave the people laws to guide them in how to worship God and how to live in the way that is right and good – a way that would be an example to all the other peoples of the world. God made a promise – a covenant: if they kept the laws, God would be their God, they would be God's people and God would take care of them.

The centuries went by. The people settled in the land they believed God was giving them and made it their home. The

The Synagogue

The synagogue is the building where Jews gather to pray together, to meet and to study. Synagogue buildings may look quite different from each other. Inside each synagogue is an open cupboard called a holy Ark (or aron hakodesh) that contains the scrolls of the books of the law. This cupboard is opposite the wall that faces Jerusalem. An everlasting light, the ner tamid, is lit near the Ark.

God told the Jewish people to make a menorah, a seven-branched gold lampstand, for their Temple in Jerusalem. After the last Temple was destroyed, it became a feature of many synagogues. This floor mosaic is from the 6th century.

great king Solomon built a temple in Jerusalem for the worship of God. Over the centuries, God sent poets and prophets to remind the people of the right way to live. Time and again, the people failed to remember God and God's laws. In the end, they were completely overrun by their enemies.

At one time, many of them were sent away to exile, forced to live far from the land they called home. There they turned back to their ancient writings, which told them of all God had done for them and what they should do to be God's people. They began meeting together on their weekly day of rest in places called synagogues to relearn everything. Slowly they put together their special books and developed the traditions of Judaism as we know them today.

The books of the Law, the Torah, are still kept on traditional scrolls protected by a scroll case. They are kept in the Ark at the front of the synagogue.

God and God's Laws

Aт тне неаrт оf тне Jеwiѕн faiтн are the laws God gave the people. The Jews count a total of 613 laws in their scriptures, but they can be summed up in ten great laws. The first four are about honouring God. The others are about treating other human beings in the right way.

Mount Sinai is the place where God gave Moses the Ten Commandments.

The Ten Commandments

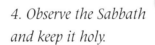

1. I am the Lord your God who brought you out of Egypt, where you were slaves. Worship no god but me.

2. Do not make for yourselves images of anything in heaven or on earth or in the water under the earth. Do not bow down to any idol or worship it.

3. Do not use my name for evil purposes.

4. Observe the Sabbath and keep it holy.

5. Respect your father and mother.

6. Do not commit murder.

7. Do not commit adultery.

8. Do not steal.

9. Do not accuse anyone falsely.

10. Do not desire what belongs to another.

A phylactery is a box, strapped to the head or arm, that contains tiny scrolls on which some of the laws are written. Phylacteries are usually worn by men and boys during prayer.

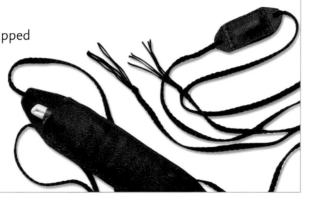

The Law and the Prophets

The book of the prophet Isaiah was written years after the time of Moses and the giving of the laws, probably when the people were forced to live in a foreign land. This was part of God's message:

The Lord says, *'Remove the chains of oppression and the yoke of injustice, and let the oppressed go free. Share your food with the hungry and open your homes to the homeless poor. Give clothes to those who have nothing to wear, and do not refuse to help your own relatives.*

'Then my favour will shine on you like the morning sun…'

Isaiah 58:6–8

Shema

The key belief of all Jews is called the Shema:

Hear, O Israel, the Lord our God is One.

Hebrew letters go from right to left, as in this handwritten version of the Shema.

The words of the Shema are the first to be whispered into the ear of a newborn Jewish baby, and the last that are said to a person who is dying.

The book of Psalms contains hymns and prayers written by different people over a long period of time. They were used by Jewish people in their worship and became part of their scriptures. This psalm shows the importance of the law for the people of Israel:

Your word is a lamp to guide me
* and a light for my path.*
Your commandments are my eternal possession;
* they are the joy of my heart.*
I have decided to obey your laws until the day I die.

Psalm 119:105, 111–112

The light from an oil lamp is a symbol of the way God's laws can light a person's way. Oil lamps similar to this one were used throughout Bible times.

Growing Up in the Jewish Faith

An important part of growing up in the Jewish faith is learning to read from the scrolls of the law, which are written in Hebrew.

At age thirteen Jewish boys have a special ceremony called a Bar Mitzvah, which means 'son of the commandment'. They have to demonstrate to everyone who gathers in the synagogue for the event that they can read aloud in Hebrew from the Scriptures. After the ceremony they are considered to be grown up.

The modern coming-of-age ceremony for girls is called a Bat Mitzvah – 'daughter of the commandment'. Girls have to be at least twelve years old before they have their Bat Mitzvah.

Living the Jewish Faith

J UDAISM BEGAN AS THE FAITH of a family – the family of Abraham. Family life is still central to living the Jewish faith.

One of the laws tells people to keep Shabbat (sometimes called Sabbath) – to keep one day in seven as a day of rest when families can relax and celebrate being together.

Shabbat lasts from sunset to sunset. It begins on Friday night, with the lighting of two candles before the evening meal. Then a blessing is said and the family shares a meal. Jewish cooks respect special laws about what foods may be eaten and the right way to prepare them. Pork, for example, is a forbidden food.

Challah is a special bread eaten on Shabbat and during festivals.

This memorial was built in Jerusalem in memory of all the children who died during the persecution by the Nazis known as the Holocaust.

The Life of the Nation

Not long after Bible times, the Jews were defeated and no longer had a land of their own. After that they lived in different countries around the world. Often they have been persecuted as outsiders. One of the worst persecutions happened in Europe in the middle of the twentieth century, when German nationalists called Nazis rounded up millions of Jews and had them put to death. A special day called Yom Hashoah has been set aside each year to remember these terrible events.

On 14 May 1948, when the Nazis had been defeated in the Second World War, the Jews had their own country again, called Israel after their ancient family name. The Jews celebrate this time with their festival Yom Ha'atzma'ut.

Saturday is the day to go to the synagogue. There will be a reading from the laws and a talk to help explain it. There will also be prayers asking for God's forgiveness and God's blessing, and the singing of psalms of praise to God.

Throughout every day, Jews try to live according to the laws: they are to be kind and fair to others. They are to take special care of anyone in need, such as the poor and the elderly. They are to respect God's world and use its resources wisely.

The Jewish faith does not have much to say about what happens after death. Whatever there is, it is in the hands of God, who is loving and trustworthy. The important thing is to live this life as God's people.

Jewish Festivals

The Jews have many festivals throughout the year.

Pesach, or Passover, happens in spring, and remembers the night in the time of Moses when God helped the people to escape from Egypt, where they were slaves.

Shavuot, seven weeks after Passover, celebrates the time when God gave the laws to Moses.

Rosh Hashanah is the Jewish new year, which happens around the beginning of October. It celebrates new beginnings.

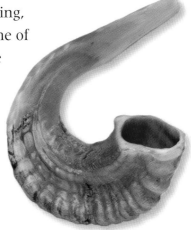

A shofar or ram's horn is blown at Rosh Hashanah.

Yom Kippur, the Day of Atonement, comes just after the Jewish new year. It is a day for asking God to forgive wrongdoing.

Sukkot is an 8-day harvest festival. People build little shelters to remind them of the time when the Israelites lived as desert wanderers – and trusted God to provide for them. The last day, **Simchat Torah**, is a happy day in the synagogue when the last story in the Torah is read aloud, and the first is begun again.

These children are playing a Hanukkah game called dreidel. Next to them you can see a hanukiah – a lamp lit at Hanukkah.

Hanukkah is a festival of lights that celebrates the rededication of the Temple in Jerusalem. It takes place in early November or December.

Purim, in early spring, remembers how a woman named Esther saved her fellow Jews from being killed.

Christianity

Christianity began about 2000 years ago.

The faith first began with **Jesus**, who is often given the title Christ (meaning chosen king).

The followers of Christianity are called **Christians**.

Their scriptures are the **Bible**. They include four books called the **Gospels**, which tell of Jesus.

Christians meet on their special day, Sunday, in a building called a **church**.

There are several different titles for the leader of the church worship, such as **priest**, **vicar** and **minister**.

The symbol of Christianity is the **cross**. Jesus was put to death on a cross, but Christians believe he rose again.

CHRISTIANITY IS THE FAITH of those who follow the teachings of someone called Jesus, who they believe is the Son of God.

JESUS LIVED AROUND 2000 years ago. He was a Jew, and he grew up in the Jewish faith. When Jesus was about thirty, he gave up his work as a carpenter and became a preacher. He called people to become part of 'the kingdom of God', living in the way that was right in God's eyes. He told people to love one another and to forgive those who did wrong, just as God loved them and forgave them.

Many people came to listen to his teaching. They also came to see his miracles: everyone was talking about how he could heal people with just a touch. Wherever they went, Jesus and his disciples were followed by huge crowds.

Throughout the ages, artists all over the world have painted pictures of Jesus. This is a symbolic picture called an icon.

Sometimes Jesus preached from the hillsides around Lake Galilee to the crowds who gathered.

The religious leaders were not happy with Jesus. They were worried that he wasn't keeping the laws correctly and was leading others astray. In the end, they plotted to get rid of him. They arrested him and told the Roman rulers of their land that he was a rebel. On a hill outside Jerusalem, Jesus was crucified, nailed to a cross of wood and left to die. Only a few friends came to lay the body in a tomb. Three days later, some of the women who had been followers of Jesus went back to the tomb. They found it open, and the body gone.

Soon after, Jesus' followers went out and about, openly spreading the same message that Jesus had preached: the news about God's kingdom, God's love and God's forgiveness.

Before Jesus was put to death he was made to wear a crown of thorns.

Jesus said people needed to become like children in order to enter the kingdom of heaven and be close to God. This picture is from a tapestry made in China.

Jesus' Teaching

Hundreds of people followed Jesus, to listen to what he had to say about God. Jesus welcomed everyone, including little children and even people who were looked down on by others.

He often taught the crowds using stories that they could easily understand but which had a special meaning. These stories are known as 'parables'. One story he told was about a lost sheep:

Once there was a shepherd who had a hundred sheep. One day he counted them and found that there were only ninety-nine: one was missing. So he left the ninety-nine safely in the pasture and looked everywhere for the lost sheep. When he found it, he brought it home and had a great party with his friends to celebrate.

Jesus explained that in the same way God does not want any one person to feel lost or alone.

Jesus' Message

There are special Bibles retold for children with colourful pictures.

The Christian Bible

Four accounts of the life of Jesus – four Gospels – are at the heart of the Christian Bible. These and a collection of letters written by some of the first Christians make up a collection they call the New Testament. The ancient scriptures of the Jews are also part of the Christian Bible. Christians call these the Old Testament.

The word 'testament' means 'covenant' or 'agreement': Christians say the Old Testament is about the old agreement God made with people through Moses – to keep God's laws. They say the New Testament is about the new agreement God made through Jesus.

JESUS WAS A JEW and belonged to the Jewish faith. He respected the old laws of his people – when someone asked him what the most important law was, he quoted the prophet Moses:

'Love the Lord your God with all your heart, with all your soul, with all your mind, and with all your strength.' The second most important commandment is this: 'Love your neighbour as you love yourself.'

Mark 12:30–31, quoting Deuteronomy 6:5 and Leviticus 19:18

But Jesus also said that he had been sent by God for something special: not to judge the people of this world about whether or not they can keep the laws faithfully, but to rescue them from their wrongdoing (John 3:17).

Christians say that Jesus is the Son of God – that he was God born into this world to live among all its wrongdoing. They say that Jesus did nothing wrong but was still put to death by his enemies. In this way he suffered the worst that human wickedness can do. When God raised him to life, he showed those who believed in him that God's love is stronger than all wrongdoing: strong enough to help people live in the right way and stronger than death itself.

Christians often read the Bible as a family and talk about what the stories mean.

The Prayer Jesus Taught

Jesus taught his followers to say this prayer. It is the most important prayer of the Christian faith and sums up Jesus' teaching.

Our Father in heaven:
May your holy name be honoured;
    may your Kingdom come;
may your will be done on earth as
    it is in heaven.
Give us today the food we need.
Forgive us the wrongs we have done,
as we forgive the wrongs that others
    have done to us.
Do not bring us to hard testing,
    but keep us safe from the Evil One.

Matthew 6:9–13

Jesus' followers believe that they should tell the world about Jesus and show God's love and forgiveness to everyone. Following the words of Jesus, they think that the most important thing is to make this world God's kingdom – to make this world a little bit more like heaven.

Jesus himself spoke of heaven: a place beyond this life where those who love God will be safe and happy for ever.

Many Christians try hard to help others in a practical way. Here, development workers and local people drill a well in a village in Cambodia.

Christians hope that death will be just the start of a new life with God in heaven.

At harvest thanksgiving services, children often say a prayer of thanks for all the good things God has given them. The food they bring is then given to people in need in the community.

Living as a Christian

A stained-glass picture recalling how Saint Francis preached to the birds.

Saints

The title 'Saint' is used by some Christians to mean someone people remember as especially holy – someone whose life inspires others and makes them want to do good things. Saint Francis, who lived in the twelfth century, is one popular saint. People often tell the story of how he gave up his riches and led a simple life, looking after the poor and showing kindness to wild animals and birds.

Some churches may use a simple goblet and loaf for sharing bread and wine; others may use a golden chalice and special wafers.

FROM THE FIRST DAYS of Christianity, Jesus' followers met together in groups to learn more about their new faith and to pray together. These groups became known as churches. Whenever someone new wanted to join, they were baptized – dipped in water as a sign of their saying goodbye to their old way of life and starting out clean and new as members of God's kingdom.

Nowadays, when Christians meet together – often in special buildings called churches – there will be teaching, reading from the Bible and prayer. Most Christians make a point of meeting each Sunday, the day of the week they believe Jesus rose from the dead. In many churches, new members are baptized as a sign of being followers of Jesus.

When a person is baptized, they are welcomed by the whole community into God's family.

Bread and Wine

One very important ceremony for Christians is the sharing of bread and wine. One of the first Christians wrote a letter to the new Christians in Corinth nearly 2000 years ago, telling them what they should remember to do:

The Lord Jesus, on the night he was betrayed, took a piece of bread, gave thanks to God, broke it, and said, 'This

The most important Christian festivals remember events in the life of Jesus.

Christmas remembers Jesus' birth.

Good Friday is a solemn day for remembering the day Jesus was crucified. It is followed by **Easter**, when Christians celebrate their belief that Jesus rose again.

Ascension remembers the day Jesus went to heaven.

Pentecost, ten days later, is about the time when God's Holy Spirit gave Jesus' followers the courage to go and spread the news about Jesus.

One Easter tradition is to make an 'Easter garden' display to remember how Jesus died on a cross and then rose again, leaving an empty tomb.

is my body, which is for you. Do this in memory of me.' In the same way, after the supper, he took the cup and said, 'This cup is God's new covenant, sealed with my blood. Whenever you drink it, do so in memory of me.'

1 Corinthians 11:23–25

As they share bread and wine together in this way, Christians remember that it is because of Jesus that they are part of God's kingdom. The ceremony of bread and wine is called different things in different churches: for example, Mass, the Eucharist, Holy Communion and the Lord's Supper.

Christian worshippers meet in this church in Guadaloupe. Many churches have a cross that is easy for everyone who passes by to see.

Islam

ISLAM BELIEVES that Allah is the One True God, and that Muhammad is Allah's prophet.

Islam was revealed in 610 CE when Muhammad first believed he was being called to be a prophet. He is commonly known as 'The Prophet'.

The followers of Islam are called **Muslims**.

Their holy book is the **Qu'ran**, and the Hadith is also an important source of teaching.

Friday is their special day.

Muslims meet in a building called a **masjid** or **mosque**.

The leader of the mosque is called the **Imam**.

A common symbol of Islam is a crescent moon and star.

Muslims believe that the Black Stone inside the Ka'bah was given to Adam by the Angel Jibril and later put it into the Ka'bah wall by Ibrahim.

THE RELIGION KNOWN as Islam began in Makkah, in Arabia, in 610 CE. A man named Muhammad lived there: he was a trader who was famous for being honest and trustworthy.

In Makkah was a building called the Ka'bah. People said that it had been a holy place from the beginning of the world but had been rebuilt by a prophet called Ibrahim – the one whom the Jewish writings called Abraham – and his son Ismail. However, by the time of Muhammad it had been filled with idols. Many of the people who came to worship there had all kinds of superstitions. But Muhammad was sincere in his faith and did not pray there.

In 610 CE, when Muhammad was forty, the Angel Jibril appeared to him and gave the first of many words from Allah, the One God. Muhammad was very frightened but, back home, his wife and cousin said they believed it was a sign he had been chosen to be a prophet.

Slowly, a few friends and family began to believe that Muhammad had something important to say and they helped to write down the words that the angel gave Muhammad. They accepted Islam by agreeing this:

There is no god but Allah and Muhammad is His messenger.

The people of Makkah did not like Muhammad and his preaching of Islam. After many hard times, Muhammad and his followers emigrated to Madinah.

While in Madinah, Muhammad taught his followers to pray facing Makkah, for he longed to return there. Eventually he and his followers did return and, from that time on, Makkah became the centre for Islam.

Muhammad made his last pilgrimage from his home in Madinah to Makkah in 632 CE. He died that same year and is buried in Madinah.

By then, after many struggles, many people had accepted Islam. Through all this time Muhammad had received more messages which his followers helped to write down. These messages were treated with great respect and eventually made into one book, the Qu'ran.

A boy visits the cave where Muhammad is thought to have been when the Angel Jibril appeared and gave him messages from Allah.

The Muslim Calendar

In the early days of Islam, Muhammad and his followers were so disliked in Makkah that they had to journey to Madinah. This journey is called the emigration or **Hijrah**, and marks the beginning of the Muslim calendar. The letters 'AH' used with the number of the year mean 'after the Hijrah'.

Jerusalem and the Night Journey

Muslims believe that Muhammad was the last and greatest in a line of prophets including Ibrahim (Abraham) and Musa (Moses) from the Jewish scriptures and Easa (Jesus) from Christian beliefs. Muslims say that in 621 CE Jibril came and took Muhammad to Jerusalem to meet the other great prophets. After this, he was taken up to heaven and back. All these events happened in the space of one night.

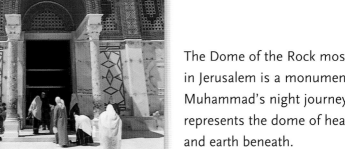

The Dome of the Rock mosque in Jerusalem is a monument to Muhammad's night journey. It represents the dome of heaven and earth beneath.

Muslim Beliefs

Muslim children are expected to read the Qu'ran.

The Qu'ran

The holy book, the Qu'ran, is written in Arabic. Muslims describe it as containing the very words of Allah. Faithful Muslims learn to read it, and many try to learn it off by heart.

Another important book for Muslims is the Hadith. This tells of Muhammad's life – the things he said and did. It was written by his companions.

The Qu'ran and the Hadith guide Muslims in the right way to live.

AT THE HEART OF ISLAM is the belief that Allah is the only true God: the creator, all-seeing and all-knowing; the One who is compassionate, merciful and forgiving. The purpose of every human being should be to serve Allah.

Muslims also believe that Allah has given clear advice to people through the prophets. They say that Muhammad was the last of many prophets, and that he brought the world the Word of Allah through the Qu'ran and the Hadith.

No one can be expected to live their lives perfectly. Only Allah is perfect, and it would be wrong for anyone to think that they can match Allah's perfection. Their aim is simply to live their lives to the best of their abilities.

Even though every human being must die, they will all be raised at the end of time for the judgment, when they will have to give an account of their deeds to Allah. The wicked will be punished, but the righteous will live in paradise for ever.

A mosaic from the Great Mosque in Damascus, built in the 8th century, shows a Muslim picture of paradise.

Angels

Muslims believe that there are heavenly beings, angels, who have been created to do what Allah requires in the universe. They believe that every person is watched by two angels who record everything that person does.

A painting dating from the 14th century shows angels including the Angel Jibril.

Words from the Qu'ran

Muhammad was dismayed at the superstitious worship of idols, and Islam forbids the making of statues or pictures showing the human face because they might be treated in the wrong way. Instead, words of the Qu'ran, in Arabic script, adorn many mosques.

Here are some sayings from the Qu'ran, in translation:

The true believers are those who only believe in Allah and his messenger. They do not doubt, but strive with their wealth and their lives for the cause of Allah. That is what sincere believers do.

Qu'ran 49.15

God is the light of the heavens and the earth... And Allah guides to his light those whom he will.

Qu'ran, from Surah 24

Muslims believe the Qu'ran contains Allah's messages to all people as revealed by Muhammad. This Qu'ran, named the Cairo Qu'ran, was made in the 18th century for the Sultan of Morocco.

Living as a Muslim

MUSLIMS MUST BE FAITHFUL in doing five things, each of them an act of worship that shows their love for and obedience to Allah. These five things are sometimes known as the five pillars of Islam.

In all things, a Muslim must be truthful, honest, respectful and kind. They must do their duty to Allah, to other people, to their community, and to the earth itself.

Among Muslims of good faith, family ties are strong and everyone is respected and cared for by the whole community.

A masjid or mosque is the place for the Muslim community to meet and to pray. Muslim men try to go to the mosque for the prayers at noon on Friday. They face a niche in one wall, the mihrab, which is built so they are facing Makkah.

Spreading the Message of Islam

A Muslim should try to spread the message of Islam to others, for they believe that only Muslims can have a place in paradise. They believe that faithfulness to Allah and right living is very important in attracting people to Islam.

Wearing traditional headscarves, these Muslim girls are studying the Qu'ran.

Shahadah

The Shahadah are words Muslims say to declare their faith: 'la ilaha ila Ilah; Muhammadun rasul allah.' 'There is no god but Allah and Muhammad is His Messenger.' As they say this, they are also saying that they will live by the guidance that Muhammad brought from Allah.

Salah

A Muslim must say the proper prayers directly to Allah five times a day, at set times. In Muslim communities, a person called a muezzin will go to the minaret of the mosque to call the faithful to prayer at the set times.

Sawm

A Muslim must fast from dawn to dusk during the Islamic month called Ramadan. To give up certain things in this way is to show obedience to Allah. It ends with the festival of Id-al-Fitr.

Cards like these are exchanged during Islamic celebrations. Id Mubarak (sometimes spelt Eid Mubarak) means 'Id blessings!'

Zakah

A Muslim believes that all one's riches really belong to Allah. A small part must be set aside to give to the things that matter to Allah. The Zakah payment usually goes to help the needy.

About two million Muslims a year take part in the pilgrimage to Makkah known as the Hajj.

Hajj

Everyone must make a pilgrimage to Makkah once in their life, as long as they can afford it without borrowing, they are well enough and the journey can be made safely. The pilgrimage ends with a festival, Id-ul-Adha, remembering the time when the prophet Ibrahim showed his complete devotion to Allah, even above devotion to his family. The festival is celebrated by Muslims all over the world.

11 Hinduism

HINDUS BELIEVE that God, known as Brahman, is everywhere and is truth.

Hinduism began over 4000 years ago.

Its true beginnings are lost in the mists of time.

Followers of Hinduism are called **Hindus**.

Their holy books include the **Vedas**, the **Upanishads** and the **Mahabharata**.

Hindus worship in a **temple**, or **mandir**, where a priest leads the ceremonies.

Hindus also worship in shrines in their own homes.

The symbol of Hinduism is the **Aum**. Aum or Om is a very special sound in Hinduism. Many claim that out of it, everything in the universe began. To say the sound is to agree that the one God, **Brahman**, truly is all in all.

Hindus believe that Shiva the destroyer can renew things in a good way. This helps people to grow spiritually. Shiva will also destroy all the worlds at the end of creation.

O F ALL THE RELIGIONS in the world today, Hinduism is the one with the longest history. There are clear signs that Hinduism existed in India around 4000 years ago; in fact, its very beginnings may be 10000 years earlier.

Hindus believe in one God who is at the heart of all there is and who is absolute truth. This one God is called Brahman.

Brahman is beyond everything but Brahman is also within everything, and the Brahman within each human being is the atman, or soul. For Hindus, heaven is when the atman and Brahman are completely one.

The sacred syllable Aum is said by Hindus during religious services and is used at the beginning and end of Hindu books. The holy symbol can also be found on many everyday objects in Hindu homes.

Three Ways of Understanding One God

The three most important ways of understanding Brahman are known as three gods: **Brahma**, the creator; **Vishnu**, the protector; and **Shiva**, the destroyer. Each one gives a glimpse of what Brahman is like.

There are many other gods and goddesses in Hinduism, but Hindus believe they are all just another part of the one Brahman. These include Ganesha, the elephant god, and Hanuman, the monkey god.

Ganesha, the elephant god, is a symbol of all that is strong and wise. Ganesha can remove obstacles standing in one's way.

Hanuman, the monkey god, is a symbol of all that is strong and energetic.

Vishnu Comes to Earth

Vishnu is a protector god and is sometimes born on earth to help put wrong things right. The person seen on earth is an **avatar**, an incarnation of the god.

One avatar of Vishnu is Krishna the cowherd who became a great soldier and a great ruler. It is partly because Krishna was first a cowherd that every cow is treated as holy among Hindus.

Another avatar of Vishnu is Rama. The story of how he defeated the demon king Ravana is told in a story-poem called the Ramayana.

In Hinduism cows are treated as holy and allowed to roam freely in the streets. At certain festivals they are often decorated, for example with bells or garlands of flowers.

Hindu Worship

Hindus gather to worship in a temple, or mandir. Gifts of flowers or food that they may bring to offer a god are later given to the poor.

A<small>N</small> <small>IMPORTANT PART</small> of Hinduism is worship, called **puja**.

Some worship is done in the temple, or mandir. A statue of a god is kept in a special room within the temple, and the priest will begin the worship there. The priest 'wakes' the god with a ceremonial bath and then dresses it in clothes and jewellery before offering flowers, fruit, sweet-smelling incense and other gifts. Then the curtains that separate the room from the main part of the temple are drawn back, and other ceremonies take place.

Some of these include singing hymns, dancing to the music of bells and tambourines and reading from the holy books. People make their offerings and say prayers. Prayers in the temple are for the community.

Most Hindu worship is done at home. There may be a prayer room or just a small place set aside. There will be a picture or statue of the chosen god or a lamp. First the worshipper washes and puts on clean clothes. Then they pray that the god who is already in the person's heart

Most Hindus have shrines in their homes with a picture or statue of their favourite deity. This is often Krishna, believed to be especially kind.

Holy Books

Hinduism is very old, and its many holy books were written over a long period of time. There are two sorts of holy books: the **Shruti** and the **Smriti**.

Shruti

Shruti means 'that which is heard'. The Shruti books are believed to come from the gods. The Vedas are hymns that were written in Sanskrit over three thousand years ago. The Upanishads are conversations between a teacher and his disciple.

From untruth lead us to Truth.
From darkness lead us to Light.
From death lead us to Immortality.
Aum Peace, Peace, Peace.

A prayer from the Vedas

Smriti

Smriti means 'that which is remembered'. These books include tales told by storytellers, such as the Ramayana (see pages 11 and 13) and the Mahabharata. The Mahabharata tells of a great war between two families – one good and the other evil. Part of it is the Bhagavad Gita or 'song of God'. This is a conversation between Krishna and a hero named Arjuna. For Hindus, this provides guidance on how to live in the way that is good and right.

This picture from the Bhagavad Gita shows Krishna (on the right) telling Arjuna the right way to live.

will come into the house and stay for the worship. The image of the god is washed and dressed or decorated. The worshipper lights a lamp and burns incense. Prayers are said and food is offered to the god before being offered to the family. There may be songs and a reading from one of the holy books. Prayers said at home are for the family and friends.

13 Living as a Hindu

Hindus often place flowers around the photograph of someone who has died. Garlands are also used to decorate the body at a funeral.

HINDUS BELIEVE that the soul – the atman – is on a journey to be as one with Brahman, like a river on its journey to the sea. This journey can last through many lifetimes. Hindus believe in rebirth: **reincarnation**. The soul leaves one body at death and is reborn as an animal or as a person, depending how they lived their last life.

The final goal – Moksha – is of being one with Brahman. There are different ways of reaching this goal.

One way is to be faithful in worship. Another is to control the mind and the body by yoga. Another – and the hardest – is to understand all the holy books with the help of a teacher, a guru.

The Ceremonies of Life

For Hindus, all of life is part of the journey of the soul. There are sixteen ceremonies called **samskars** marking stages in a person's life. The first two are before birth. The third happens when a baby is born: the Aum is marked on their tongue with a golden pen dipped in honey. The last is the funeral, when the body is cremated. The Ganges river in India is thought to be holy, and if the ashes can be lowered into the Ganges at a place called Varanasi it is believed the atman will have reached its goal.

Hindus believe that several rivers in India are holy. Many will make the journey to wash in them, to receive a special blessing. These pilgrims are washing in the River Ganges, a big river that flows across India.

The fourth way – the way of **karma** – is very important. Karma is the law of cause and effect. Bad deeds have a bad effect and tie the body to life on earth as a lowly creature. Good and kind deeds bring a person closer to the end of the journey. As a result, Hinduism teaches non-violence – no fighting or killing. Many Hindus are vegetarians.

Hindus are accepting of other faiths and believe that there are many paths to know the one God, just like the many paths up a mountain. Despite different starting points, people may find at the top that they share the same view and the same understanding.

Hindu Festivals

There are many festivals in Hinduism. Most Hindus celebrate the ones that are linked to their favourite gods.

Divali, the festival of lights, is one of the best known. It happens in October or November and is celebrated with the lighting of lamps. It is said that the goddess of wealth, Lakshmi, visits each home where lights are burning and brings good luck.

At Divali Hindus also celebrate the time when Vishnu, the protector, was born as Rama. The Ramayana tells how Rama's beautiful wife Sita was kidnapped by a demon and was rescued by Rama.

Holi celebrates Krishna's visit to earth as an avatar of Vishnu. Holi is celebrated in spring.

At Divali, Hindus light candles to invite Lakshmi, the goddess of fortune, to visit.

Buddhism

BUDDHISTS TRY TO ACHIEVE enlightenment through the way they live, and perfect peace.

Buddhism began in the sixth century BCE with the teachings of someone called **Siddhartha Gautama**, who became known as the **Buddha**.

The followers of Buddhism are called **Buddhists**.

The **Pali Canon** is one of the great collections of special writings in Buddhism.

Buddhists worship in **temples** and also at shrines in their own homes.

The symbol of Buddhism is a wheel with eight spokes, reminding followers of the **Eightfold Path** to enlightenment.

BUDDHISM BEGAN WITH one person, Siddhartha Gautama. He was born a prince in a tiny country in what is now southern Nepal. His father wanted him to be a warrior king like himself, and he kept his son in great luxury in the grounds of the palace where he learned the skills of a warrior. When he was sixteen, he married a beautiful princess, and they lived happily together for thirteen years, during which time they had a family.

Everything seemed perfect, but Siddhartha was growing more curious about what lay beyond the palace. In the end he demanded to be allowed out to see the kingdom.

First Siddhartha saw an old man. He was shocked to realize that he would not be a young man for ever. Next

In his search for wisdom, Siddhartha nearly starved himself, and all his bones showed through his skin.

When Buddhists worship, either in the temple or at home, they often show reverence to the statue of Buddha and then say prayers.

he saw a sick person and realized he would not be strong for ever. Then he saw a corpse in a funeral procession and realized he would not live for ever. All this made Siddhartha deeply depressed until he saw someone who looked serene and happy: a holy man, a beggar monk.

Siddhartha set out to learn wisdom. At first, he too became a beggar monk. Then he found another teacher who encouraged him to live a very simple life with no comforts. Siddhartha starved himself almost to death, but then realized that this was as useless to gaining wisdom as the way of luxury.

Other holy men mocked him as he left them to live a gentler life – not too little for the body and not too much – and set off to find wisdom by himself. He went and sat in the shade of a fig tree and there he believed he finally understood the answer to the problem of suffering in the world. He became 'fully awake' to reality: he became the Buddha, the 'enlightened one'. He began to teach others, including the monks who had earlier mocked him. They became the first disciples of the Buddha, the beginnings of a community of monks – the Sangha.

It was while Siddhartha was resting under a bodhi or fig tree that he gained enlightenment. The tree is also known as the Tree of Wisdom.

This is a picture of the enlightened Buddha. Most Buddhist temples contain impressive statues of the Buddha.

Buddhist Beliefs

At the heart of the Buddha's teaching are what he called the **Four Noble Truths**:

1. At the heart of everything is suffering (dukkha).

2. Suffering exists because people are always wanting things. In fact, they are never happy with what they have.

3. Suffering ends when people let go of the wanting.

4. To get rid of suffering, people must follow the eightfold path.

Prayer flags are often used in some Buddhist countries. Here they are tied to a stupa, or shrine, to celebrate the Tibetan new year in the Kathmandu Valley in Nepal.

Nirvana

Buddhists believe that nothing in the world lasts for ever – everything is locked in the cycle of birth and death like the pattern of the seasons. Wishing that things were for ever is at the heart of this world's suffering. Following the path to enlightenment can free the person from this pattern of suffering and release them into a place of perfect peace: **nirvana**.

Beauty can rise up in unexpected places, like this flower. In the same way, Buddhists believe that people can rise up from the world's suffering and find peace.

The Eightfold Path to Enlightenment

Followers of the Buddha, the Enlightened One, are themselves on the path to enlightenment, beyond suffering. The first two steps require wisdom:

1. Right understanding: understanding the Four Noble Truths.

2. Right thoughts: a commitment to live in the light of the Noble Truths with love towards others.

The next three require morality:

3. Right speech: pure and kind, avoiding gossiping, lying and angry words.

4. Right conduct: doing good and showing loving kindness.

5. Right livelihood: choosing work that is peaceable and does no harm to living things.

The last three are linked to meditation, which is a central part of Buddhism:

6. Right effort: making a conscious effort to get rid of bad thoughts and replace them with good ones.

7. Right mindfulness: being aware of oneself and of the needs of others.

8. Right concentration: learning to meditate and become calm and peaceful.

A young boy meditates at the Buddhist Dharma School in Brighton, England.

A raindrop inspired this Buddhist saying:

This life is as the tiny splash of a raindrop: a thing of beauty that disappears as soon as it comes into being.

So set your goal clearly and make right use of every day and every night.

Tibetan Buddhist proverb

Five Promises

The five promises or precepts are rules of good behaviour that all Buddhists try to follow:

1. I will not harm or kill any living thing.
2. I will not take what belongs to others.
3. I will not indulge the body.
4. I will not lie or gossip.
5. I will not drink alcohol or take drugs, which cloud the mind.

Buddhist monks and nuns make extra promises.

Living as a Buddhist

Buddhists wear different types of ceremonial headdress. This young monk comes from Qinghai Sheng, in China.

Holy Books

There are two main branches of Buddhism and they each have their own holy books. **Theravada** Buddhists believe that the teachings of the Buddha were handed down by word of mouth long before being written down nearly five hundred years later in the language of Pali. Their holy book is called the Pali Canon.

    Mahayana Buddhism has books that were first written in Sanskrit. Much of what is in them is very like the Pali Canon, but there are also writings by other Buddhists who achieved enlightenment.

THE BUDDHA WAS NOT A GOD, and Buddha did not teach that there was any god. Even so, Buddhists set aside places to bow before a statue of the Buddha – in monasteries, in temples and in shrines in the home. Worship involves meditation, listening to teaching, chanting and making offerings.

Many Buddhists have a statue of Buddha such as this one in their home, which is usually kept in a special room for worship called a shrine room.

Buddhist Festivals

In November, Buddhists celebrate the Floating Candle Festival. Candles are put in tiny cups made out of leaves or paper and floated on a river.

The birth, enlightenment and death of the Buddha are all said to have happened in the same month of the year, Wesak, which falls in May or June. Buddhists decorate their houses and temples with many candles, the light being a sign of enlightenment.

May you be filled with loving kindness.
May you be well.
May you be peaceful and at ease.
May you be happy.

Tibetan Buddhist blessing

The Three Jewels

Buddhists give thanks for the three key things that help them in their faith, known as the Three Jewels:

1. The Buddha.

2. The Dharma – teaching that includes the Four Noble Truths, the Eightfold Path and other special writings.

3. The Sangha – the community of Buddhist monks and those who have achieved enlightenment.

Many Buddhists join monasteries to study and pray, and live a simple spiritual life in a community. Some stay for a short time; others for life. Here two young Buddhist monks at a monastery in Tibet go about their daily tasks.

Sikhism

SIKHS BELIEVE IN ONE GOD, who is in everyone and is everywhere. Living as a community is very important for Sikhs.

Sikhism began about 500 years ago when a man called **Nanak** believed he was being called by God to be a religious teacher – a guru.

This is an important Sikh of today wearing traditional dress and carrying a sword.

The followers of Sikhism are called **Sikhs**.

Their holy book is the **Guru Granth Sahib**.

Sikhs meet in a building called a **gurdwara**.

The symbol of Sikhism is called the **Khanda**. It is made up of a straight-edged sword, a ring and two curved swords. These represent God's power, justice, truth and infinity.

SIKHISM IS BASED on the teaching of someone known as Guru Nanak. The word 'guru' means 'teacher', and the word 'Sikh' comes from a word meaning 'disciple'.

Nanak was born in 1469 CE in a place that is now part of Pakistan. His family were Hindus, and even as a child he seemed to be unusually thoughtful and wise. He liked to spend time talking to the various travelling holy men who came by. Some were Hindu and some were Muslim, so he learned about both faiths.

One day, when he was thirty, he was bathing in the River Bein when he felt himself being carried up to heaven. He was missing for three days and his family thought he must have drowned, but then Nanak came back and said that God had called him to be a guru. He himself became a travelling holy man, preaching both to Hindus and to Muslims. After twenty years, he settled down in the Punjab region as a farmer. Soon disciples came to join him. This was the first community of Sikhs.

The Ten Gurus

Before he died, Nanak chose someone to be the next leader of the community. This person became the Guru Angad. He wrote many hymns.

The third Guru was Guru Amar Das. He built the first langar – a kitchen for all the community so that everyone who came could share a meal together.

After him came Guru Ram Das. He founded the holy city of the Sikh faith: Amritsar, in North India. The fifth Guru, Guru Arjan, built a beautiful temple in the middle of a lake there. He also wrote hymns and put them together in a book with hymns by earlier gurus. This was called the Adi Granth, the 'first book'.

Next came Guru Har Gobind, Guru Har Rai and Guru Har Krishan. By the time of the tenth guru, Guru Gobind Singh (1675–1708), life had become very difficult for Sikhs. Guru Gobind Singh set up the brotherhood, the Khalsa, in which men were trained to fight with swords to defend themselves.

Guru Gobind Singh was the last person to be called a guru in Sikhism. He declared that the holy book, the Adi Granth, was to be the Guru, or teacher, ever after. It became known as the Guru Granth Sahib. The new words show that the Granth, the book, is to be treated as a highly respected teacher.

This is a picture of the ten Gurus who were so important in developing the Sikh faith. Each one chose the next to follow him. In the centre is the founder of Sikhism, Guru Nanak.

18 Sikh Beliefs

Sikhs believe it is important to think about God – sometimes they sing hymns or listen to readings from holy books, or just sit quietly on their own.

AT THE HEART OF THE SIKH FAITH is the belief in one God. This God who is beyond everything is also within each person. By saying the Nam, the name of God, and meditating on it, each person can know God more and more. They can also learn to live this life as God wants, treating everyone as equal, and loving and serving one another.

In this way, each person can break out of the cycle of reincarnation – of being born again and again in different forms. They will find enlightenment, knowing they are one with God. This is called nirvana.

The Community of Sikhs

The tenth Guru, Guru Gobind Singh, set up a community of Sikhs, the Khalsa. In his day, this community was a brotherhood of men who were willing to fight to defend

---

Mool Mantar

The first statement in the Guru Granth Sahib is called the Mool Mantar, which is a declaration about God:

There is only one God. Truth is his name. He is the creator. He is without fear. He is without hate. He is timeless and without form. He is beyond death, the enlightened one. He can be known by the Guru's grace.

ੴ
There is only one God.

ਸਤਿ ਨਾਮੁ
Truth is his name.

ਕਰਤਾ ਪੁਰਖ
He is the creator.

ਨਿਰ ਭਉ
He is without fear.

ਨਿਰ ਵੈਰੁ
He is without hate.

ਅਕਾਲ ਮੂਰਤਿ
He is timeless and without form.

ਅਜੂਨੀ ਸੈਭੰ
He is beyond death, the enlightened one.

ਗੁਰ ਪ੍ਰਸਾਦਿ ॥
He can be known by the Guru's grace.

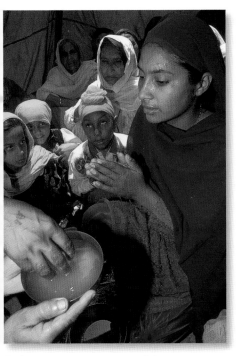

At her amrit ceremony this young girl becomes a full member of the community.

their faith. Nowadays, the community includes men and women as equals.

They agree to follow strict rules in order to serve God: they agree to recite hymns five times a day, to abstain from alcohol and drugs, to be faithful in marriage, to be honest, to serve others and to help the poor.

There is a joining ceremony at which a new member drinks a special sugar water, called amrit.

Every male in the community takes the name Singh, which means lion. Every female is called Kaur, which means princess.

The Five Ks

There are five things that show a person is a member of the Khalsa. They are called the five Ks.

Kesh Members of the Khalsa do not cut their hair or shave their beard.

Kirpan This is a sword, to show that the person is willing to fight to defend their faith. Nowadays, this is often a small symbolic sword.

Kangha A comb, used as part of keeping oneself clean.

Kara A steel bracelet. This round circle is a reminder that the link between God and the person is unbreakable.

Kachera These are traditional shorts. Wearing them is a reminder that everyone should be dressed ready for action in defending the faith.

When these boys grow up they will become members of the Khalsa.

Living as a Sikh

This service in the gurdwara shows the Guru Granth Sahib on cushions under a canopy. Anyone is allowed to read from the holy book.

THE SIKH PLACE OF WORSHIP is called a gurdwara. The word means 'the guru's gate'. A gurdwara is often quite plain. The holy book, the Guru Granth Sahib, is kept raised up on cushions and under a canopy. People cover their heads, remove their shoes and come and sit on the floor as a sign of respect. They listen to a reading from the book and sing hymns.

After the service, everyone goes to the kitchen, the langar, to share a meal. There is special food called karah parshad, made with flour, butter, sugar and water, to remind people of the sweetness of God. Everyone is welcome.

Sikh Festivals

Sikhism has its roots in Hinduism, and some of its festivals are very much the same.

At Divali, for example, people put many lights in the gurdwara to remind them that God is the light of all the world and of their lives.

Special celebrations called the gurpurbs remember the ten Gurus. There are processions and ceremonies in the gurdwara. Everyone is invited to a meal in the langar, even if they are not members of the community.

Sikh women prepare food in the langar, the open kitchen.

The Golden Temple in Amritsar

Many Sikhs visit the Golden Temple in the city of Amritsar in North India. It is in the middle of a holy lake and connected to the mainland by a causeway.

The temple is built out of marble, covered with gilded copper and inlaid with precious stones.

It has four entrances, to show that it is open to all God's people. On the outside there are verses from the Adi Granth, and inside the temple are pictures of Guru Nanak and his followers.

Each morning, the Guru Granth Sahib is carried on a silver casket along the causeway to the temple. During the day, worshippers read constantly from the holy book. At night-time it is taken back to the treasury, where it is guarded until the next morning.

The temple in Amritsar has been known as the Golden Temple ever since it was rebuilt in marble and covered with gilded copper at the beginning of the 19th century.

The Difference a Faith Makes

Religion can be like a light that shows people the way to live and helps them make decisions.

RELIGIOUS PEOPLE OFTEN SAY that their faith is like a light. It helps them understand the mystery of life; it provides the belief that life has a purpose. It also shines a light on what is right and what is wrong. Their understanding of right and wrong affects the choices they make about how to live their lives.

Belonging to a faith can also provide people with a special community. Some believers may actually join a community and live there. Many others continue living in the everyday world but have a network of fellow believers whom they meet when they go to worship and who care for one another in all the ups and downs of life.

Many religious people find comfort in their faith in bad times, and they hope and trust that God can make good come out of bad.

Problems with Religion

For religious people, doing what is right really matters, and that can lead to good things, such as concern for peace and justice however long the struggle.

Sometimes religious belief does not appear to be a good thing because it seems to lead to extreme behaviour. People can become very passionate about their beliefs because these beliefs are linked in their minds to things of everlasting worth. Indeed, they become so passionate that they lose sight of the values at the heart of their faith.

For example, hundreds of years ago, people in Christian Europe began to think it was very important that they should control the land where Jesus lived. They went to war to drive the Muslims out of Jerusalem and other places in the Holy Land, and the wars – the Crusades – caused great suffering.

People of good faith within each of the main religions are dismayed at some of the actions of extremists.

The Baha'i House of Worship in New Delhi, in India. The Baha'i faith is one of the newest major religions of the world and has its roots in Islam. Baha'is hope for a united world of peace. This temple is a place of prayer open to people from all faiths.

The Humanity We Share

Through history and still today, religious faith has inspired many people to deeds of shining goodness.

At the same time, there are people who claim to have no religious faith who also show great kindness and compassion, and who risk their lives to bring peace and justice to the world.

There are many values that both religious people and non-religious people can share, including the importance of respect and tolerance for one another because we share a common humanity.

Believers also enjoy sharing traditions and festivals together. These help mark the pattern of the year and the passing of the years, giving shape to their lives.

For many religious people, their faith is especially important when they come face to face with the fact that nothing in this world lasts for ever, that people die, and that they themselves will one day die. Each of the great faiths provides an understanding of what is of everlasting value.

Mother Teresa was a Christian nun who became famous throughout the world for helping the poor people on the streets of Calcutta in India. She inspired many people to do similar work, showing love and kindness to those in need.

Index